100 RULES

FOR
THE NEW BODYGUARD

– Part One –

100 RULES FOR THE NEW BODYGUARD - PART 1
Copyright © 2023 by Mark Phillips.

PTC publishes in a variety of print and electronic formats and by print-on-demand. Some material included with standard print versions of this book may not be included in e-books or print-on-demand. If this book refers to media that is not included in the version you have purchased, you may download this material at http://www.bodyguards4hire.com

FOR INFORMATION CONTACT:

Email: info@ptc.services
Website: www.ptc.services/permissions

Book and Cover design by: © 2023 Phillips Technical Consulting, LLC. ISBN: 978-1-7333677-0-7
Library of Congress Control Number: 2019910593
Published by Phillips Technical Consulting, LLC. Deerfield Beach, FL

First Edition: 2023

Phillips Technical Consulting, LLC 906 SE 11th Ave.
Deerfield Beach, FL 33441
www.ptc.services

ORDERING INFORMATION:

Special discounts are available on quantity purchases by corporations, associations, educators, and others. For details, contact the publisher at the above-listed address.

U.S. trade bookstores and wholesalers: Please contact Phillips Technical Consulting, LLC Tel: +1.863.333.5350 or email at info@ptc.services.

DEDICATION

This book is dedicated to each bodyguard who gave their lives in service to a client or principal. Your sacrifice and the sacrifice of your family do not go unnoticed.

Contents

FOREWORD

There are some people who are born protectors. Who when trouble arises - runs toward the problem, not away, to ensure the safety of all involved. Big Mark the Bodyguard is one of those people.

Literally, from the day we met, I have observed Mark protecting others. I've learned from him as we worked countless details together. We co-founded BODYGUARDS DETROIT and BODYGUARDS4HIRE.COM, worked tirelessly for our clients, trained bodyguard courses and grew our business to the #1 Bodyguards Service in the United States with a 100% success rate.

If you are considering a career in protections, if you are also a natural protector, or if you just want to know what it is like to work near and around celebrities, top executives, and the wealthy, then you will find this book valuable. Why try to navigate this exclusive industry alone? In this book, Mark shares with you easy-to-apply advice to help you decide what type of training you need, how to work with clients, where to secure details and develop clientele, as well as health and wellness strategies to prepare you for the work which requires physical and mental toughness. In Part 2, which I have had the privilege of early access – He continues setting you up for success by digging into protection strategies, tips, and tricks to set yourself apart in the industry and much, much more.

On a personal note, there is no one who could be prouder to watch their business partner and husband share his depth of knowledge and experience with each of you. I have always felt completely safe in Mark's presence and much safer when navigating this world based on all I have learned from him over the years. I have watched Mark masterfully navigate this industry's challenges and because of his leadership we have secured an amazing clientele, worked with industry elite, been on concert stages, television and movie sets, walked red carpets, and more. Big Mark the Bodyguard is a thought leader, public speaker, and a true influencer for the protections industry. Adding author to that list is a natural progression. Mark, your vision and unyielding perseverance has taken us on such a wonderful adventure. I can't wait to see what's next for us! If I told you the sky was the limit you would find a way to get us to the stars!

Your loving wife,

LaToya Phillips

CEO of BODYGUARDS DETROIT & BODYGUARDS 4 HIRE

PREFACE

Daily, our company receives phone calls and inquiries from interested individuals looking to join the elite network of bodyguards at our company, Bodyguards 4 Hire. Some have a security, military, or law enforcement background. Many are just starting out.

I have enjoyed a successful career as a celebrity and corporate bodyguard. Due to my experience and expertise, I've enjoyed working with the elite, the famous (sometimes infamous) and being mentored by those who set the bar for celebrity protection. The goal of "Bodyguards 4 Hire: 100 Rules for the New Bodyguard – Part 1" is to answer the question: "What does the new bodyguard need to know before getting started?" There is much to learn about the protections industry. And if you are trying to determine your career path, you may not be ready to travel across the country and invest in pricey courses just to find out if this is the right industry for you. This book will save you both time and money all while providing a foundation for you to build your career in protections upon.

WHY SHOULD YOU READ THIS BOOK?

Of course, I am biased and think you should read this book. However, you could benefit from reading any reference book that focuses on the protections industry. So why read this book? Bodyguards 4 Hire: 100 Rules for the New Bodyguard – Part 1 isn't focused on theory. Rather, it contains real- world tools, techniques and exercises which make a huge difference in your ability to apply what you read. Within these pages, you will find numerous straight-forward examples which relate to each specific topic and questions that will help you to retain and apply each concept and how it can be used in the real world.

HOW TO READ THIS BOOK

The 50 rules in this volume have been grouped together based on topic. You don't have to read this book cover to cover, nor completely in sequence. If you need to know more about a specific topic, use the contents page to find your way directly to it. We want you to be able to apply the direction and advice as you need it and refer often to benefit from the practical wisdom you have at your disposal. The terms client and principal are used interchangeably throughout the rules to represent the person or people being protected.

Within some rules, we may offer additional digital products – free to you for purchasing this book. You will find links to those products, so that you may always access the latest and greatest versions.

And that's it. I hope you enjoy and benefit from the first half of the rules written specifically for you!

Mark Phillips

Author
COO of BODYGUARDS DETROIT & BODYGUARDS 4 HIRE

THE BODYGUARD & TRAINING

An empty training room that could be used for bodyguard training.

RULE 1: GET TRAINED

A common concern of those entering the bodyguard industry is whether or not to invest in training courses, and if so, what school would be best suited to you? One reason to consider attending one or more training schools may be that the industry constantly changes. Every year, there are changes to the laws in various states and countries and you may not know where to look in order to identify and meet the requirements for the profession in your area.

Often these schools travel from town to town offering this training and occasionally various organizations will collaborate to conduct classes. This, however, can be very expensive. Some schools can cost in upwards of $5000 or more when you factor in hotel, food, flights, equipment, learning tools, etc.

If you're just starting out, you may not be able to afford the cost of attending a bodyguard school. This leaves the select few who can truly afford to attend these pricey courses. Upon completion of the course, these new graduates may now have greater access to employment opportunities because they have been able to afford a seat at the table.

Another way to gain valuable experience and exposure is to offer to intern with a recognized / reputable protections company or a well-known bodyguard in the industry. It doesn't make much sense to spend money you don't have yet.

If there's a class available to you at a reasonable cost and instructed by those qualified to teach, then you may consider trying it out. You may make lasting associations during training with your instructors and classmates, but a class rarely guarantees future work. The decision is up to you. But if you choose not to attend one of these schools, don't worry - we've got you covered.

In Bodyguards 4 Hire: 100 Rules for the New Bodyguard: Part 1, you will receive the basic information you need to know to take your first steps into the industry. Before you get started, sign up today for our mailing list at Bodyguards4Hire.com for additional unique training opportunities. If you were one of the first to purchase this book, you will receive discounted rates on your first course.

HOW WOULD YOU ANSWER?

Why do you want to become a bodyguard?

_____

How will this book help you on this journey?

_____

Aircraft hangar filled with private jet and a luxury sport vehicle.

RULE 2: THE GLAMOUROUS LIFE IS FOR THE PRINCIPAL

Congratulations! You just recently accepted your first bodyguard assignment and are now looking forward to jet setting around the globe, protecting the rich and famous. You can hardly control your excitement as you await your first deployment.

You arrive to work the detail and are briefed. The principal will be speaking at a fundraising event to be held at a prestigious hotel and conference center in the metropolitan downtown area. One by one your team members receive their post. Now, it's your turn. The team leader assigns several men and women to remain in close proximity to the principal. Some are placed in positions where they can conduct surveillance of the audience and others in high visibility areas to deter any attacks. The team leader is about to open his mouth and issue your orders but when he does you can hardly believe your ears. In a low and confident voice, he utters, "Guard the rear exit door. "You assume that he must've misspoke, so you ask that he repeat himself. He does so but repeats the same sentence this time with even more confidence. "Guard the rear exit door."

You think surely this must be a mistake. You didn't travel all the way there to guard a rear door! But, once again the team leader assures you that he indeed placed you at the back door that can only be accessed from the inside by going through the hotel's kitchen. This assignment positions you far from the event and the attention of the principal. What's more is that you aren't going to be placed inside the kitchen where it is warm but on the other side of the door in a dark alley and guess what...It just started raining.

So, the event begins, and you are alone, wet, and livid. The only thing that you have to lessen the blow of your solitary confinement (so-to-speak) is the two-way radio chatter in your ear from the rest of your team. You begin wondering why the team leader hates you so much and what could you have possibly done to irritate him. Four hours pass by, and you are still there. What a terrible start to your career.

This illustration demonstrates how many new bodyguards may perceive varying assignments. Basically, any assignment that places you outside of the direct and close proximity of the principal may cause resentment. Why? Not many who decide to take the steps necessary to enter the prestigious ranks of the bodyguard industry will want to be placed in another room while all the lights, cameras, and action are taking place elsewhere.

Just like everyone else, bodyguards greatly enjoy the excess that results from their access to the corporate executive, Ultra High Net Worth (UHNW) individual, or celebrity principal. It's usually the team leader who is seen in the media walking with the principal. What goes unseen is the many other bodyguards just outside of the camera shot.

It is usually the team leader that gets into every event or exclusive restaurant. And it will usually be the team leader that will get approached for future work independent of the team. The bodyguard assigned to be the closest to the principal will certainly shine brighter than you. It's very difficult to beat that when you're standing outside with the SUVs, tour buses, in an alley, stairwell, kitchen, or dressing room. But make no mistake, you manning that post is very important. If it wasn't, then no one would be assigned to it.

The profession of bodyguard has its high points and its lows. One minute you're on a private jet with an A Lister and then the next moment you're at the county fair protecting a singer that was a "One Hit Wonder." It won't all be champagne bottles, supermodels, award shows or even steady long-term assignments. This business can be tough and very competitive. The last thing you want to do is not perform in a professional manner because you dislike the assignment. Word gets around fast between clients and your fellow bodyguards. Your reputation must be built and good or bad it will take time.

FEEL BETTER, WARM SOUP IS HERE

You are right where you need to be. Before you can take over the industry, you need to first learn what the industry intel is and why. Learning every position, post, and station on an assignment is the quickest way to demonstrate to others that you are ready for more responsibility.

A team leader may post you in a certain location to gauge your willingness to follow direction and monitor your progress. The bodyguard that is willing and determined to stand firm in an alley during a thunderstorm to contribute to the safety of the principal and the effectiveness of the team is the bodyguard who will one day direct a team of his own.

I encourage you to learn everything you can about this industry. Selecting this book of rules was a great start. Continue selecting my books and who knows? In just a little while you may be well on your way to sampling the glamourous life.

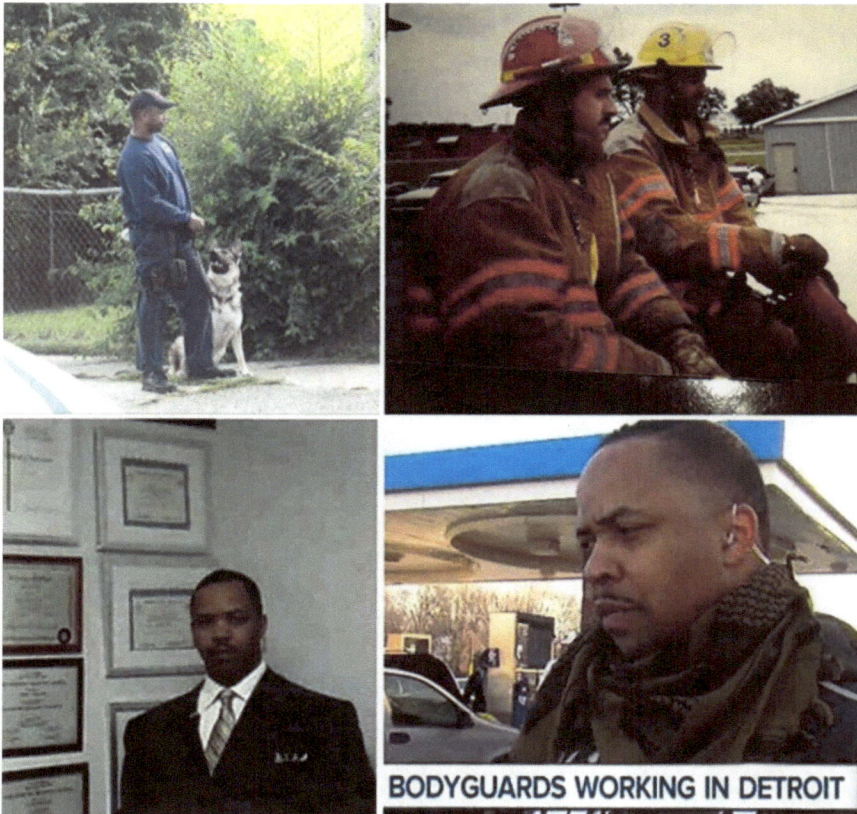

Big Mark the Bodyguard standing next to a wall displaying some of his licenses and certification as well as in many work scenarios.

RULE 3: KNOW WHAT LICENSING & CERTIFICATIONS YOU'LL NEED

Depending on where you operate, there may be licensing, and/or certification requirements required by the government in that area. For example, in the State of Florida, USA those working in the security industry are required to attend certain security training courses to obtain a certificate of training before applying for a security license. There are different licenses that one might desire, so there are different certifications you may need to qualify for each respective license. Again, this will vary depending on where in the world you live or operate.

Some places do not regulate the bodyguard industry at all. There may even be certain locales that offer reciprocity to those who have registered companies from these locations. Check with your country, state, or city government to determine the applicable licensing and certification requirements. This also might be done quickly with an internet search. Some certification classes can be as short as a few hours and others considerably longer.

RESEARCH & LIST THE LICENSES REQUIRED FOR YOUR AREA

_____

_____

_____

_____

_____

_____

An operative with his weapon in the field.

RULE 4: BE MORE THAN A HIRED GUN

For as long as I can remember, various tactical weaponry has been a part of the bodyguard ensemble. Many schools for the education of bodyguards feature training courses related to firearms use and other weapons tactics. Various dignitaries and Heads of State utilize law enforcement, military, and private defense contractors to carry out the task of protecting them, and they too have received extensive firearms and weapons training. Now comes a reality that most don't discuss.

One issue that every new bodyguard must consider is whether using a firearm or weapon to conduct business as a bodyguard is necessary or not. As a protection specialist, you may be asked to work in all sorts of situations and environments. But there are many countries, states and venues that do not allow bodyguards to carry weapons of any kind unless they have permission from that specific government. This can prove to be a headache for you and your client. Many clients/principals will not know or care about the difficulties associated with you carrying or not carrying the weapons that they may have specified that you indeed possess. This will be especially difficult for the bodyguard new to the industry or even the protections specialist who hasn't done much traveling.

Take for example: You're driving your principal to a casino. You park or valet the vehicle and proceed into the building with the principal. You come to a gaming area entry checkpoint and the metal detector goes off. The staff there advises you that you are not allowed to bring your weapon into the venue according to local laws and corporate policy. You are asked to leave the casino and secure your weapon elsewhere before you return.

Your principal is eager to go into the gaming area and get their evening started. But certainly, you're not going to allow your high value principal to go ahead unprotected, so you insist that they accompany you back to the vehicle. The principal is highly annoyed that you are stopping the fun that they came there to enjoy. I'll stop the illustration here. At this point, you have:

- Irritated the principal.
- Given the principal good reason to believe you didn't do any advance and you are incompetent.
- Possibly ended your principal's night before it ever began.
- Wasted the principal's money (transportation, your services, etc.)
- Possibly gotten yourself fired.
- Ensured that you won't get a recommendation.
- Tarnished your reputation as a bodyguard.
- And so on...

Here's a fact contrary to what you may hear in many training courses. You can't take a firearm or other weapons with you everywhere. So, you must wrap your mind around that fact now. Make adjustments in how you operate. It may not be wise to leave your firearm in a gun box you've placed in the vehicle you arrived in, because the vehicle or the firearm can be stolen. You must learn to rely on more than your weapons to have longevity in this business. You must adapt to the environment that you find yourself in. If the casino doesn't allow you to carry a gun, then that's the environment that you must adapt to.

Don't be labeled a "hired gun."

One thing I detest from an employer's standpoint is when a possible hire candidate calls and the first thing out of their mouth is information about their formidable array of firearms. I want to hear about more than your guns. I'm not saying that you can't exercise your legal rights where they apply. What I am saying is be flexible and adaptable. Be more than muscle and guns. A well-rounded resume includes practical training, certifications, licensing, and experience. The stereotype of the gun-toting bodyguard has plagued our industry for far too long and today can limit the type of clients you attract. Today you can be the change we need.

HOW WOULD YOU ANSWER?

What skills do you have to defend yourself or your client that does not require a weapon?

_____

What skills could you further develop?

It is important to know the laws pertaining to our industry.

RULE 5: KNOW YOUR BODYGUARD LAW

One of the most important things that a professional bodyguard must know is the law as it pertains to this business. Year after year those calling themselves bodyguards, security guards, bouncers, and doormen are arrested, sued, and even given lengthy prison terms because they assumed that the law was on their side. It is beyond important that you have not only a knowledge of the laws related to this profession, but also how to apply the laws in a working environment.

Here's the reality. For almost every law that says that you can legally do something as a protection professional, there's several other laws that can be applied that say you can't. This can become a living nightmare for the inexperienced bodyguard. You've taken all the required courses, received your certifications and licenses to qualify for work, but just like a police officer who just completed academy training, there's additional on-the-job training that may be required. Cops learn how to apply their new knowledge by working with a Field Training Officer who helps them deal with the realities of the job that they can't get in a controlled environment like a classroom. You, the bodyguard also need that kind of training.

Reading this book is just one of many steps you'll need to take to protect both your principal and you. Knowing the difference between a choke hold and a sleeper hold and whether either can be legally applied is just one more issue you'll need to resolve before you can even think about applying one or the other. Additional legal issues like whether you're required to obtain business insurance and what kind or if you can even afford it may discourage even the most dedicated bodyguard. It is also very unfortunate that many well-known bodyguard training schools will charge anywhere from $1000 to $10000 for the training you need to gain a grasp of the legal requirements you must meet in order to begin to be profitable and safe from prosecution.

It is ultimately your responsibility to understand the law and other factors that may impede your progress. Knowing things like, many police officers moonlight as bodyguards or security personnel and may see anyone that's not a member of law enforcement as a rival or threat to their income. Some with varying backgrounds may feel that you're not nearly as

qualified as they are to deal with threats, nor do you have the authority to.

While these matters have no real basis in law, you may still have to deal with them if you find yourself in a legal battle. Knowing your legal authority to perform your job in the city, county, state, or country that you operate in is crucial to avoiding what could be the start of a bumpy legal outcome.

Look up legal statutes related to this profession in West Law, or other legal journals or contact an attorney who specializes in winning self-defense cases. There are several cases on the legal books that demonstrate clearly how a paid security professional, bodyguard, is required to defend those under his care instead of fleeing for safety. Become familiar with these various case laws. A prosecuting attorney is not likely to tell you that you had the legal right to defend yourself and others. Instead, you may be likened to a vigilante, thug bouncer with no training, or a violent rage monster. As for judges and juries, they may understand little about the laws, statutes, and legislative intent regarding our profession. So, it's up to you to know what the law requires of you, and how to navigate it to survive.

FREE LEGAL RESOURCES

www.lexisone.com
www.findlaw.com
www.westlaw.com

Will you be a professional or thug bodyguard?

RULE 6: KNOW WHAT KIND OF BODYGUARD YOU WANT TO BE

So, you might be asking yourself, what in the world is he talking about?

In this industry, you will find that there are many origin stories. Some came into the business after completing a career in the military or law enforcement. Many worked for several years in a security (guard) capacity. Others started out as night club bouncers or even bathroom attendants. There are also those who ended up earning the trust of their employers with no background at all.

The only real difference between them all at the end of the day is how they got started and their success rate. Don't overly focus on any of these factors. You've already taken the best step by reading this book.

If you don't have training, get some. If you need experience, seek some. If you think it matters more whether or not you obtain a certificate from a security or bodyguard school, then you're wrong. The network and reputation you build are what lasts. Establish yourself in this business and none of your competitors can determine your future.

Often the bodyguard who has no formal security or protections training - but is tall or muscular - may be considered the thug bodyguard by those who have received formal training from a reputable school or organization. The THUG BODYGUARD employed by the client or principal and has proven himself on the job may at times be the one tasked with finding additional well-trained individuals to supplement the protections staff. So, never be overly critical about the working experience and background of others in the industry who have already proven themselves to their clients. You never know how well connected they may already be. So never be too judgmental, it may just hinder your ability to secure more work and do damage to your professional reputation.

HOW WOULD YOU ANSWER?

You are approached about working a protections detail. How would you describe your professional experience?

_____

_____

_____

THE BODYGUARD & THE PRINCIPAL

At times you may be asked to do tasks other than protections.

RULE 7: BECOME A TRUSTED RESOURCE

If you are finding your way into the ranks of trained and working bodyguards, I encourage you to take note of this topic. Whether you want to be referred to as a bodyguard, close protection specialist, executive protection specialist or any of several other titles you may apply to yourself, there is one thing you should consider. Are you a bodyguard or a servant?

When participating in many training courses you may hear instructors insisting that you cannot and will not do anything in the performance of your duties that resembles that of a servant for your principal. Instructors can be very insistent that you can't protect your client effectively and carry his or her shopping bags, walk pets, or run errands. You may hear how doing so tarnishes the industry and may set a new standard for how bodyguards are perceived by clients.

It has been my experience that you must display flexibility concerning this issue. Certainly, you want to keep your principal safe, but you also need to keep them happy or at least as happy as you can within reason. The bodyguard that regularly tells his/ her principal "No" at every little request may not have a principal to protect for very long. There needs to be some balance. Whether a short detail that lasts a few hours or one that lasts for years, you could be asked to carry out many tasks not directly related to the training that you've received. I have had principals ask me to shine shoes, cock meals, shop for them, handle booking their shows, contribute musically to studio sessions, and even conduct financial transactions for them and their families. No matter what the task I never viewed the request as an insult to my professional standing or a threat to their safety. I wisely accepted one truth "my principal trusted me".

When your principal gives you these tasks, they are simply saying that they trust you. They may rely on you more than anyone else in their circle of close associates. You are the one who is with them more often than others so why shouldn't they entrust you to take on more responsibilities.

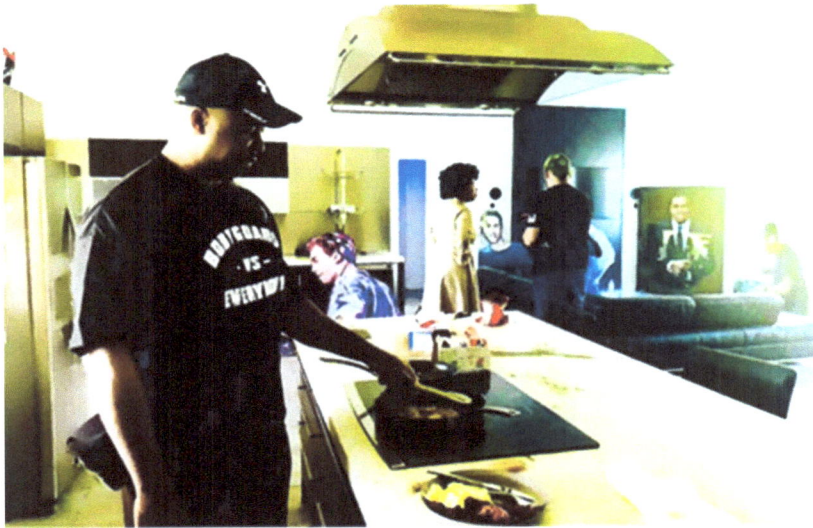

Big Mark making breakfast for a client at a Florida recording studio.

A client or principal that asks you to carry out multiple tasks may be grooming you for a greater title than that of protector (I have known several bodyguards working in the entertainment industry
who because they were found to be reliable, were later offered positions as business manager, road manager, and personal or executive assistant. More about that in rule #8!)

Some bodyguards, because of their unwavering dedication to carrying out almost any task requested of them by the principal even gained some measure of celebrity of their own. THE NEW KIDS ON THE BLOCK, Will Smith, and Steve Harvey are just a few celebrity entertainers whose bodyguards went on to secure fame and wealth for themselves with the assistance of their principals.

So, when I hear bodyguard school instructors, and course developers, tell their students that they shouldn't ever get coffee for the principal or carry shopping bags it raises a Red Flag! I challenge you to take a moment and search the internet for celebrity bodyguards. I am

35

confident that you will find a good number of reputable bodyguards carrying bags and walking dogs. These are the bodyguards that secure long-term assignments and command large salaries or rates, as well as other perks. Your instructors themselves may be amongst those whose images appear on the web or social media carry bags and scooping dog poo.

The reality is that some training schools for bodyguards may make it a practice of charging you extremely high cost to attend their class or course only for you to be taught the opposite of what will make you a profitable bodyguard. Know this, that if an instructor is an active bodyguard, then he may also be your biggest competition. Would it be in their best interest to show you how to compete against them? That's for you to decide. There are few instructors that have enough business of their own that they don't need to compete against others. I'm one of them.

Remember not to sell yourself short. Always make sure that the safety of your principal is a priority but be ready to become more than a bodyguard. Be ready to become a valued asset to your client and in turn launch your career to heights you never even considered.

HOW WOULD YOU ANSWER?

It is best to predetermine what you will or will not contribute as a member of a professional detail. What skills or services would you be willing to offer clients outside of their physical protection? Make a list below.

_____

_____

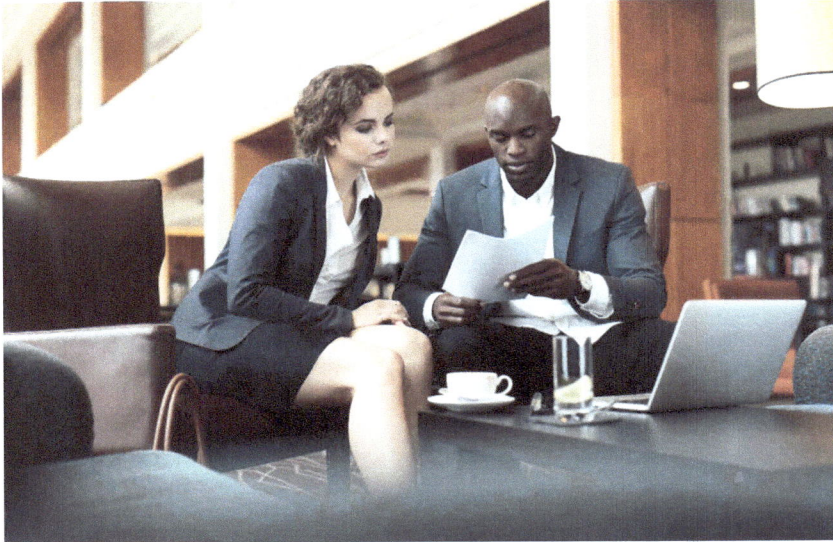

As relationships evolve so does your role with the client.

RULE 8: NAVIGATE CLIENT RELATIONSHIPS CAREFULLY

The business of being a professional bodyguard is just that...a business. You may start your career as an employee of a security or protection agency. Each of these companies will have rules and requirements for its employees to follow. Failing to follow these policies and procedures may result in a suspension of employment, job termination, poor reputation, and possibly the loss of a paying client to your employer. So be very careful to follow the rules that you agree to. Always make an effort to maintain professionalism with the company's client.

On the other hand, should your crossover into the ranks of the independent contractor or head up your own team along with your own clients you may have a lot more freedom in how you conduct yourself. The exceptional bodyguard functioning as an independent contractor will work diligently to develop strong professional ties with his or her principal.

As mentioned in rule #7, over time some bodyguards and their principals develop mutual respect and even admiration which can lead to a more personal bodyguard-client relationship. Some bodyguards because of their dedication and ability to not only do the job of protecting the principal but also taking on many other responsibilities have been offered additional duties and titles to include:

Band Manager

Agent

Tour Manager

PR Rep

Business Manager

Spokesperson

Security Director

Not everyone will have the exact same experiences over the course of their careers. Some protection specialists move into the above-mentioned positions because they were already friends with the principal and after some time learning the ropes of the job they are offered a new role. Some are just likeable and easy to work with. While others are well educated and have prior experience.

What I'm trying to say is that there is no one right way to do this job. There are, however, many wrong ways to do it. What works well for one bodyguard and principal won't work for another. In my younger years I was a straight arrow. I was determined to be a professional robot on the job, never letting my hair down so to speak.

Not under any circumstance would I deviate from my training. I can honestly tell you that not every principal appreciated that. If you're on a long-term assignment you may see your principal every day. On the special days when they walk the red carpet, win awards, close a big deal, or when they travel the world performing for tens of thousands of their adoring fans, you're right their behind them keeping them safe from harm or delay. So, it's not so unusual for the client to befriend you the bodyguard and expect that when no one else is looking that you let your hair down for a second. Sometime your principal may be dealing with a lot of stress and require a listening ear. Other times the two of you may be abroad and the principal falls ill and you must watch over them until their health is restored. The principal will usually let you know when they require such attention from you.

███████████████████████████████

IMPORTANT THINGS TO REMEMBER...

Should friendship with your client sour, it could mean the end of your assignment with that principal or any potential work with their associates.

Sometimes, the wealthy, the powerful, and the celebrity may be used to getting their way. This is usually because they are surrounded by people that are perfectly fine with telling them that they are right, even when they clearly in the wrong.

If you are a Type A/Alpha personality and used to being a straight shooter who speaks his or her mind, and you become a friend to your powerful client, you may want to share your actual opinions on matters unrelated to their protection. You may find that your contributions are not always well received. So be wise in your conversation and cautious not to become distracted from your main purpose.

Big Mark managing a protections detail where law enforcement was utilized.

RULE 9: LEARN TO LIAISON WITH LAW ENFORCEMENT

There are very few individuals or organizations today that have conducted the business of executive protections and not had to work closely with law enforcement. If your principal is famous enough, you may find the local authorities providing motorcade escorts, supplementing your protections staff, and offering faster response times. Whenever you and your staff are preparing for larger or more visible details, it may prove to be wise to notify local law enforcement in the areas that you are working in.

There's not much worse than being professionally embarrassed because the police were called on you or your team because someone noticed a group or individual with weapons dressed in black moving back and forth in an area. Notifications to law enforcement can be simple or complex but can clear up a misunderstanding before it becomes a problem. This might be done by calling a department's dispatch line or simply going to the police station and explaining what you are doing. Be respectful and professional.

Also keep in mind that in some states, law enforcement oversees licensing requirements for those working in the Bodyguard industry and they don't always allow for reciprocity. So, if you're not licensed in that state or country you may have to check that "Bodyguard" title at the door for one of concierge, event services rep, or assistant. Whether or not to contact local law enforcement should be established by whoever is leading the protections detail and the principal or their representatives prior to engagement. For big awards shows, a lot of these logistics may already be handled.

Some police departments have liaison officers who deal with various organizations or an executive protection division that can be hired through the department to assist. Be sure to develop a good relationship with these department representatives. They might offer advice and assistance that you otherwise wouldn't receive. These relationships can last the length of your career.

If you for whatever reason believe that notifying anyone outside of the protections detail might delay or hinder the operation or principal, you may decide not to make notification at all. Consider this carefully. It could be the difference between having all the support in the world or being road blocked.

WHAT TO INCLUDE WHEN A LIASON

When acting a liaison with law enforcement, include:
- Organization or team being represented
- Identity of the principal client, if required
- Duration of the detail
- Basic detail logistics
- Team attire

Discussing protection needs with a corporate client.

RULE 10: ADJUST WHEN WORKING WITH CORPORATE CLIENTS

Providing services to a corporation can vary. You may be assigned to protect anyone within an organization - from the valued employee up to the CEO. So, you don't always assume that you are going to be jet setting and wearing fine, tailored suits. Sometimes you may be posted in a lobby, office, or moving from one location to another.

Not all corporate clients are alike. Some executives are down to earth and friendly while others require that you never speak directly to them, unless necessary. Be ready for whatever comes your way but do so with a professional appearance and good conduct.

Do your homework. Just because you made it through the door doesn't mean they will tolerate anything less than excellence. Determine what business qualifications must be met to provide services to the organization. Many larger corporations may require you to meet certain industry standards, so be ready when the Big Boys Call. It could mean the difference between struggling to gain new clients and having more than you can handle.

LARGE CORPORATIONS MAY REQUIRE:
- Registration of your organization with the state
- Business licensing and certifications
- Workers' compensation insurance
- Business insurance specifically for bodyguards (and LOTS of it)
- Large commercial vehicle insurance policies
- Business mailing address
- Company website
- Verifiable, relevant recommendations
- And more...

Learn the likes and dislikes of your celebrity client.

RULE 11: UNDERSTAND THE CELEBRITY CLIENT

Celebrity clients and principals can also vary widely. Some celebrities are new to show business and others have been established for a long time.

The personality of each celebrity client is unique. Prior to the detail, always do your homework to determine what they may require of you and/or your team. You may have to initially deal with a manager, agent or other representative before coming in contact with the celebrity principal. Make sure to show due respect and maintain professionalism.

What if the celebrity requires additional services that are not included in your service agreement? There are plenty of bodyguards that refuse to go outside of the scope of work. An example may be that the principal wants you to walk the family dog around the block. Walk the dog or not - things like this should be established prior to accepting the assignment so as not to waste either party's time. If you have problems with getting a latte for the boss, then you definitely won't want to be walking a dog and picking up his droppings.

Seriously, be ready for anything if you are dealing with a celebrity. Especially if they are an A-lister! Have a current passport, credit cards that aren't maxed out, etc. You never know when they may need you to step in and save the day, in another capacity other than protector.

Some bodyguards gain a celebrity following because they have the credentials and the abilities necessary. Others may know the right people. There are often those who get the good jobs just because they are big as a house! Celebrities and those who represent them can sometimes prefer big people movers. So, whether you are a giant or James bond, be prepared to be the best or someone else will.

And most importantly never behave live fan. Always be professional.

KEEP IN MIND...

A celebrity client's activity may differ. An entertainer's itinerary may differ to that of a best-selling author or public figure. Be versatile and ready to adapt based on the client. Ask questions of your team leader to determine the best way to provide service.

A celebrity making an appearance at a night club.

RULE 12: BE CAUTIOUS OF NIGHT CLUB APPEARANCES

Depending on where you are, a night club appearance can be a great experience or a serious tragedy.

Night club appearances can be conducted at large upscale venues with professional security personnel in place or secluded and tight buildings in the middle of bad neighborhoods. Whether or not your client/principal chooses to make an appearance at either place isn't always up to you. Often a club appearance may come directly after a concert performance by your principal hence the title of "after-party". Club and concert promoters may pay a performer or influencer anywhere from $1,000 to $100,000 for as little as a half hour appearance or to stay and be visible for the whole night.

Personal appearances by your client can often times offset the cost of his or her touring, monies owed to a record label, or other costs. It would not be prudent to assume that you can convince a principal or their team that it's not worth the trouble to honor a paid request to appear at a night club especially after agreeing to do so.

A thing to remember when you are protecting an entertainer, or any other public figure, is if they don't get paid, oftentimes neither do you. Now that that's been said, you still must make the best recommendations to your client or team leaders regarding everyone's safety. Planning travel routes, advancing, and other exit strategies are still a must to help ensure the protection of all parties.

Get to know the staff at the venue/ club especially the security staff. Winning the security staff over may allow you to gain extra bodies to cover gaps in your detail. This may also endear you to the security staff and help prevent internal plots and schemes to undermine the protection of both you and your principal.

Examples of how quickly things can go wrong at any venue, hotel, or night club are as follows.

- Yung Berg (Attacked and Robbed) Detroit, MI
- Christina Grimmie (Shot & Killed) Orlando, FL
- Jay Z and Beyoncé (Stage Breach) Atlanta, GA
- Ariana Grande (Bombing at Venue) Manchester, England
- Kim Kardashian (Attacked, Kidnapped, Robbed, several times) Paris, France
- And many others.

This task may always prove to be a thorn in your side. Your Principal, You and Your Team may travel to countries where there is civil and governmental unrest, and you may be uncertain about the roads,

▶ celebrity life

The Voice singer, Christina Grimmie, shot dead while signing autographs after concert

THE family of the gunman who killed Voice singer Christina Grimmie left a message on their front door expressing their "sorrow" over his actions.

AP · News Corp Australia Network · JUNE 11 2016 9 50AM

The Voice US Season 6 contestant Christina Grimmie is in a critical condition after being shot at a concert venue in Orlando. Picture: Robb D Cohen/Invision. Source: AP

THE FAMILY of a gunman who shot and killed a rising singer penned a note addressing the tragic incident.

The family of killer Kevin James Loibl posted a note on the front door of their St Petersburg home, expressing their "deepest sorrow" for the loss "to the family, friends & fans of the very talented, loving Christina Grimmie".

They ended by saying there would be no other comments.

No one answered the door to the one-story house, which had a rusted metal animal trap in the yard.

Article-source:

https://www.news.com.au/entertainment/celebrity-life/the-voice-singer-christina-grimmie-shot-while-signing-autographs-after-concert/news-story/ea4c39a16e6658f433a016288c860318

the people, or even the authority's ability to assist you if something goes wrong. Night club appearances present a real risk that you must

51

consider. Be determined to pay close attention to those who support your goal of keeping your client safe and of those who do not as you may end up returning to that location again someday.

AT ANY VENUE TAKE VERY SERIOUSLY THE FOLLOWING:

- Determine whether you have an adequate number of protections team members for your detail.

- Advance ahead of the detail to identify routes and threats.

- Prepare travel routes and alternates in the event of traffic delays or detours.

- Identify entrances and exits.

- Compensate for lighting or lack of.

- Assess the staff at venues.

- Monitor the size of the crowd and determine if it is being managed safely.

- Monitor any suspicious individuals or groups.

- Gather information about possible attacks.

- Address the lack of venue security with internal team.

- Determine the best placement of your vehicle(s) and driver(s) in case a fast departure is required.

Wherever your principal may take you, be vigilant in your efforts to keep them and others safe and make allies you can rely upon. It may mean your life and that of those you protect.

WHAT OTHER THINGS SHOULD YOU CONSIDER?

Thinking about the venues in your area. What other precautions could you take to keep a client safe?

_____

_____

_____

A bodyguard who had to deal with a difficult client.

RULE 13: BEWARE OF THE DIFFICULT PRINCIPAL

In the world of personal protection, you may quickly find out that you are not in control of everything that you were told that you would be in a bodyguard training program. Some principals may refuse to take any of your recommendations no matter how reasonable. Others may seem to purposely put themselves and their entourage in harm's way.

The successful people that you'll find yourself working for didn't get to the level of success that they currently enjoy by letting other people tell them what they can and cannot do. The list of advisors counseling them on where they can and can't go now includes you.

Your principal may be extremely busy running their business enterprise which in turn provides the financial means to support many of their family members, employees, and friends. A missed appointment because of a recommendation by you can result in a loss of what could be millions of dollars for your client and your abrupt termination from the protective detail.

A GOOD SOLUTION:

Before recommending that your principal miss an appointment or a curtain call, be sure that your recommendations are based on valid intel and credible threat assessments.

Maintaining flexibility will allow you to make the appropriate adjustments in your security planning and improve your ability to strategize in a pinch. Being too rigid when it comes to the protection of your principal and those around them will only cause alienation. Keep in mind your principal is a human being with varying emotions, responsibilities, and beliefs which may differ from what you're accustomed to.

By finding mutual ground with those you protect, along with having the right motives, you may improve your ability to convince your principal that the course of action that you recommend is in their best interest and allow for a more pleasant work environment.

THINGS TO REMEMBER

- The principal is a human being with thoughts, emotions, responsibilities, and belief systems
- The principal may be responsible for not only their well-being but that of their family, employees, business partners, and vendors
- As their bodyguard, you must ensure that intel is valid, threats are credible, and your security plan is well defined

55

Bodyguard restricting access to their client.

RULE 14: BE READY TO BE THE BAD GUY

Here's another truth about becoming a personal bodyguard. If your principal requires it, you may be asked to be the "BAD GUY' so that they can save face and be seen as the good guy.

"What does he mean by that?" you may be asking.

Imagine you and the principal are at a business conference where he or she is the keynote speaker. People are lined up to speak with your client. Because your principal is a very busy person and couldn't possibly speak to everyone present, they may ask you to step in and interrupt, giving them the opportunity to walk away gracefully without insulting anyone.

This action will usually be planned to make sure you and your principal understand various cues to follow. Some principals may display a certain hand gesture to signal to you in the event they find themselves in trouble or should they no longer desire to speak with a particular individual, cueing you to step in.

Others may offer a glance or specific time period for each encounter with a guest. No matter what the signal may be, the other parties involved may see you as the one who stole an opportunity away from them. You, however, can show only a small amount of sympathy to them by offering a brief apology for interrupting before whisking your client away.

The "BAD GUY" is necessary to keep your client on schedule, deter unwanted advances, and keep them from becoming an exposed target to attacks by lingering in one place for too long. The mild discomfort that some new bodyguards may display because of performing this task should dissipate over time as you take more and more pride in knowing that your principal remains safe in part due to your diligence in performing this required task.

As time goes on, the dedicated bodyguard will develop a keen skill at interrupting conversations between a principal and another individual. In fact, the personal bodyguard is one of the few professions where the employee/ contractor can interrupt the boss at any time...even while speaking publicly to an audience if the interruption is warranted.

So, take pride in becoming the "BAD GUY". After all, lives are at stake.

HOW WOULD YOU ANSWER?

Your principal has just signaled you to interrupt a conversation they are in. What would you do?

_____

_____

_____

Big Mark on the red-carpet protecting recording artists.

RULE 15: BE READY TO FALL BACK

So now you're a bodyguard. You protect the biggest celebs and corporate moguls with honor. You're finally in the big leagues and you love it. You should certainly feel a certain level of pride and self-importance for all you have accomplished. You spend many hours with your principal while he or she conducts business, enjoy leisure and even family time. Your principals' spouse(s), children and friend(s) may even consider you a part of the family makeup. There's no doubt in your mind that you not only are a valued member of your principal's inner circle but that you are good friends.

Now one fine day you are conducting business as usual protecting your principal at an industry function. Your principal has been in your care for an extended period of time now (let's say 6 continuous months). You're having a private conversation with your principal like you do every morning when an important associate of your client walks up and interrupts you mid-sentence almost as if you weren't standing there.

At this point you and many others may have your own opinion on how to deal with what seems like a simple issue. So how would you handle this situation?

BIG MARK THE BODYGUARD

Would you:

a. Tell them you and your principal are busy.
b. Invite your principal's associate to join you in the conversation.
c. Excuse yourself from the conversation allowing your principal and their associates to speak privately i.e., Falling Back.

Each of the above choices may seem reasonable, but in the world of executive and personal protection it would be wise to choose answer C). Often celebrities, public figures, and high-ranking corporate executives have images to maintain or must treat their associates like VIPs as a matter of conducting business and increasing revenue. That becomes more difficult for your principal if you, the bodyguard, aren't willing to play ball so to speak.

Always be polite and professionally minded when bowing out of a conversation. Your client will certainly appreciate your effort to make their life easier.

FOOD FOR THOUGHT

Put yourself in your client's shoes. There may come a day when you need to cease conversation with a member of your team because a potential client, colleague or a pressing matter needs to take precedence. Always remember to display humility while keeping your client safe.

THE BODYGUARD & BUSINESS

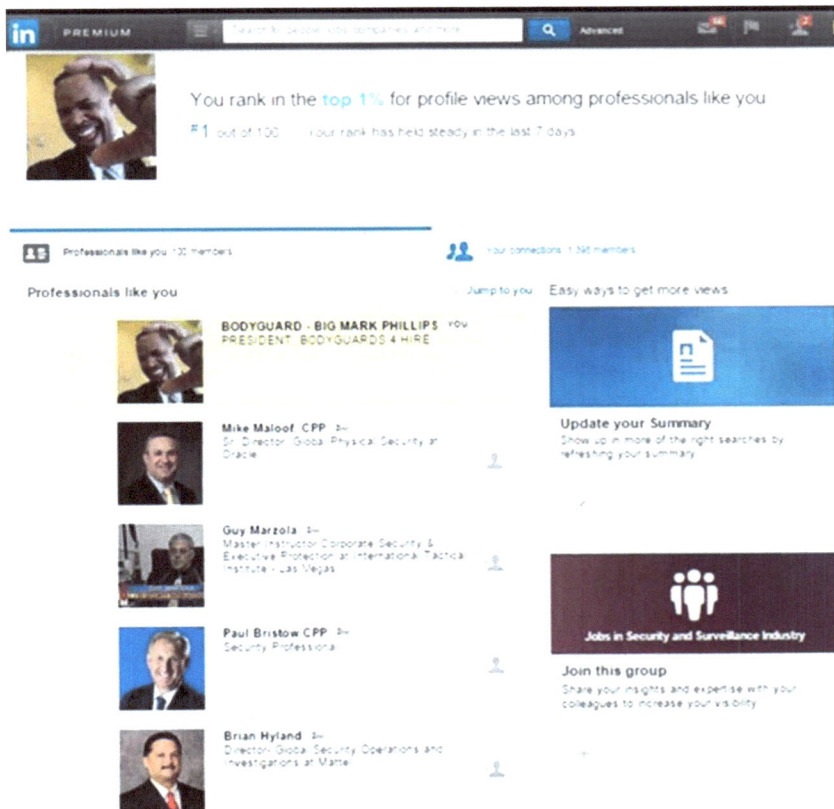

Customer referrals, LinkedIn rankings, and mentor recommendations can help establish your reputation.

RULE 16: GET VETTED

When clients are considering which bodyguard or bodyguard service to utilize, they often times take into consideration recommendations from friends, family, associates, and acquaintances. In other words, your reputation can and should proceed you.

However, when you're new to this business that may prove to be difficult when you haven't had a chance to build one yet. Some examples of individuals who may enter this industry with a reputation already intact are former college, and professional football and basketball players, bodybuilders, military, and members of law enforcement with dignitary protections experience. If you do not however have this background, you probably won't be easily found on the radar of those seeking a bodyguard.

Even if you do formerly hail from one of these professions, you will have plenty of competition to contend with. Your experience may not be the same as that of an experienced and recognized bodyguard.

The bodyguard that doesn't have a full resume of experience and/or training may benefit tremendously from being mentored and vetted. Those with a depth of experience, who are respected and known in the industry, can verify your skills and abilities and have great influence with potential clients looking to verify your qualifications. Speak with as many people as you can to gauge for yourself which organizations would be the best fit for you and the career you want to build.

In a profession where lives can and will be on the line every day, the bodyguard that can prove they are who and what they say they are will advance much faster than their counterparts.

I recommend that you make your services available to more than a few bodyguard and security agencies to increase your exposure to multiple opportunities.

Be open to constructive criticism. You may not always agree with the direction you receive, but that doesn't mean that the advice won't be beneficial. In time, you may find that you have all the recommendations that you need when potential clients and employers call.

Someday, it might be you that's doing the vetting.

A bodyguard verifying the validity of a client.

RULE 17: VERIFY THE CLIENT AND THE DETAIL

The bodyguard working for a security or protection agency may routinely receive his assignments from his superiors with little thought as to the legitimacy of the client's request for service or client identity.

Some agencies intentionally withhold this information from its employees due to confidentiality requirements from the client, or even the threat that employees may attempt to win the client over for themselves if allowed to have access to that information. But now you are an independent bodyguard or maybe you own and operate an agency of your own. The responsibility of verifying the identity of all potential clients and the legitimacy of their request for services falls on you. Why might this be of concern, you might ask?

It has been my experience that not every request for protective services is a legitimate one. Your phone may ring often with you anticipating the next well-paying gig. However, what you may find on the other end of a phone call, email, our website request are competitors scoping out your business, the mentally ill, criminals looking to hire thugs, and the immature playing pranks.

You may even receive requests from those with real threats, but who should be contacting local law enforcement for help and not a bodyguard. Often, I get these requests from individuals who have no way at all to cover the cost or expenses associated with hiring a bodyguard. Many refuse to give real names, locations or details of the threat, nor will they offer any means of payment.

Be very careful when you receive requests for detailed information about your professional licenses, rates, insurance coverage, and company operations from those not yet verified. The person on the other end might just be a competitor looking to cause you trouble.

By taking measures to determine the validity of any request, you will avoid wasting time and resources.

WAYS TO VERIFY YOUR NEW CLIENT
- Complete a preliminary application
- Request identification
- Utilize search engines
- Search for relevant news articles
- Explore social media
- Use identity verification services

Be sure to set appropriate pricing.

RULE 18: ESTABLISH YOUR PRICING

Many worry too much about what their competitors charge, and not enough about what their clients want to pay. Determine what your skillset is worth and what that should cost. If you are not turning a profit or at least ensuring return business, then you may not be charging enough. Offer additional services, when possible, to sweeten the deal and maybe they will pay you what you think is deserved.

It is not recommended that you wait until you arrive at an assignment to work out payment, especially if you haven't established a previous work history with that client. Do not be surprised if a client skips out on paying you what was agreed upon if you haven't established billing procedures that allow you to collect what is owed to you. This is impossible if you don't implement a billing standard or practice. Be ready to justify your rates and expenses as well as knowing the difference between the two. Your rate is the dollar amount that you will be paid for protections services. This is usually hourly or a flat rate. Accepting only a rate may cut you out of being paid the various expenses that you will need to operate effectively.

EXPENSES MAY INCLUDE:

- Travel time and other travel related expenses

- Admission into venues

- Mileage

- Report writing

- Lodging (Hotel)

- Vehicle allowances

- Required equipment purchased or rented for the assignment

- Per-diem

- Additional expenses may vary.

Please take this rule seriously. If you don't, you may find those clients who attempt to skip out, never paying you for your services or expenses. It is a hard lesson to learn, but you need not experience it if you take the needed steps to protect yourself. The exact method you use is up to you. Do your due diligence.

SERVICES YOU CAN USE TO COLLECT PAYMENT
- PayPal
- Square
- Venmo
- CashApp
- Apple Pay
- Google Pay
- Due
- Authorize.Net

Two businessmen making an agreement.

RULE 19: CLOSE THE DEAL

This will be a simple rule. No client or principal is the same and applying the same method to win them over every time most likely won't work. An experienced bodyguard may utilize photos and videos of themselves working with various A & B List celebs to convince a potential client that they're the right one for the job. Others may present letters of recommendation from past clients along with related credentials.

Still others may have networked their way into the job via someone they know. There are even some who don't have to try to win a new client over. Their large size or reputation may do it for them. No matter the way you gain the interest of a prospective client, convincing them to hire you is finally accomplished when you've both agreed upon your rate and money is deposited into your bank account or pocket.

Happy hunting.

HOW WOULD YOU ANSWER?

What is the best way for YOU to close the deal?

_____

_____

_____

_____

40% of business revenue comes from repeat customers.

According to SumAll Analytics, 40% of business revenue comes from repeat business.

RULE 20: CLOSE THE DEAL-MOVE FROM CUSTOMER TO CLIENTELLE

It is one thing to be hired for a temporary protection detail.
It is another ball game entirely to convince a previous client to utilize your services either repeatedly or exclusively. Simply do your best. Should you find yourself assigned to working with a team, make sure to hold one another accountable. So often bodyguards let down their guard and become too relaxed after crossing over into regular work for a client.

HERE IS A SCENARIO:

The protection detail went very well, or so it appeared. But what went unnoticed by many was that 'one bodyguard 'who made unwelcome advances on an assistant to the principal while others were grabbing gift bags meant for the guests.

The principal nor their staff ever said a word about it to the team leader. The team was just never contacted again. The only reason any of this was made known to the team leader was that they overheard the principal discussing it with the staff.

This would've likely been a long-term detail with a very wealthy principal willing to pay the desired pay rate. What a shame that the entire detail lost out because all but a few were professional. Your principal crossing over from customer to client means that they are now repeat business and out of everyone else they chose you. Maintaining that client is crucial to a good reputation. Poor conduct on your behalf may result in the word being put out that you can't be trusted.

A good report can result in more business for you or your company from the principal's associates. Do your utmost to please your client/ principal so that you can enjoy a long and profitable protection detail.

SELF REFLECTION

What steps can you take to increase repeat work opportunities for you and the teams you join?

_____

_____

_____

_____

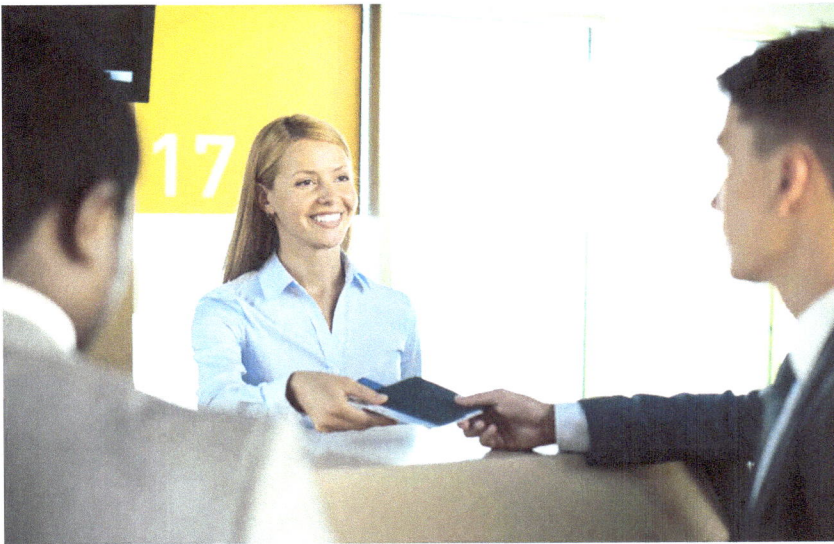

Bodyguard presenting his passport to an airport representative.

RULE 21: BE PREPARED TO TRAVEL

Before you can travel with you principal, you must be sure of several things. Every bodyguard should have appropriate identification to travel domestically and abroad. Having a passport, driver's license or any other necessary documents will help things go smoothly.

Also, be prepared to apply for expedited screening checks from the various government agencies worldwide to get you and your principal to your mode of travel faster by being able to expedite the security screening process. You don't want to find yourself in a situation where your principal will not have you by their side because you are stuck at a checkpoint.

There are a few options in the United States that can help with this concern, including GLOBAL ENTRY, VARIOUS VISA, TSA, PRE CHECK, NEXUS CARD, etc.

Do your research and determine which of these options is best for your travel needs.

HERE'S A TIP

If for some reason, you are unable to travel domestically or abroad, resolve the issue or make your team leader aware. This may exclude you from some details, but it will prevent your team leader from committing you to an assignment only to have to replace you and update the client later. Being honest here will further add to your credibility.

Establish a contractual agreement.

RULE 22: ESTABLISH A CONTRACT

Before starting any assignment, it is always best practice to have a clear understanding in writing between you and your client as to your specific responsibilities as a bodyguard.

This should also be established when acting as an independent contractor for a bodyguard service.

The contract is a statement of work which clearly states the scope of your duties and limitations as it relates to the detail duration, pay rate, expenses covered/not covered, travel, etc. This contract also makes the client aware of their responsibilities. This statement outlines what will ensure the success of the detail as well as what would cause the detail to fail. This needs to be established and agreed upon before any work is started and both you and your principal need to agree on every term. Why is this important? Because in the unfortunate event that something goes wrong the contract and statement of work will be the legal document used to determine liability.

A bodyguard should request this document from the client as proof that they are a hired professional performing their duties to protect someone. This document can be submitted by you to your client to fill out, or it can be issued to you upon request from the client. Either way, anyone working a protections detail would be better protected by having this document in their possession.

RESOURCE

You can download free contract templates here:
https://www.smartsheet.com/free-statement-work-templates

A *non-disclosure and non-compete agreement is essential.*

RULE 23: ESTABLISH NON-DISCLOSURE & NON-COMPETE AGREEMENT

The protections industry is very competitive and often you may find those you've employed are looking to make your clients their own - and for less money. It might be done as simply as passing a business card or making a sales pitch. This is a concern to the industry because it can drive down rates. Before you know it, no one is earning what they should because enough unprofessional people undercut the very ones who attempted to assist them with their career.

Establish boundaries from the start. Make sure it is understood that your staff, whether direct or contractor, should never approach your clients, principals, their families, or associates for future work. It may even be necessary to advise your clients to keep you informed of any attempts to go around you. To avoid this, a non-compete and non-disclosure agreement may be required.

A non-compete agreement binds employees and contractors from competing against their employer for work with new and established clients and their affiliates. It deters your employees and contractors from making any attempts to steal the client for themselves.

A non-disclosure agreement bars employees and contractors from sharing various details about a specific client. These documents are vital resources used to deter anyone from disclosing any information that should not be public knowledge.

Should you prove to be successful in this business, you too may require those employed or contracted by you to agree to the terms of a non-compete and non-disclosure. There are very few things in this industry worse than securing work only to be double-crossed by a member of your own team. A document of this sort is a legally binding agreement, so it is recommended that you read it carefully. Possibly even consult a legal professional before agreeing to its terms.

RESOURCE

You can download free non-disclosure and non-compete agreements at: https://www.nondisclosureagreement.com

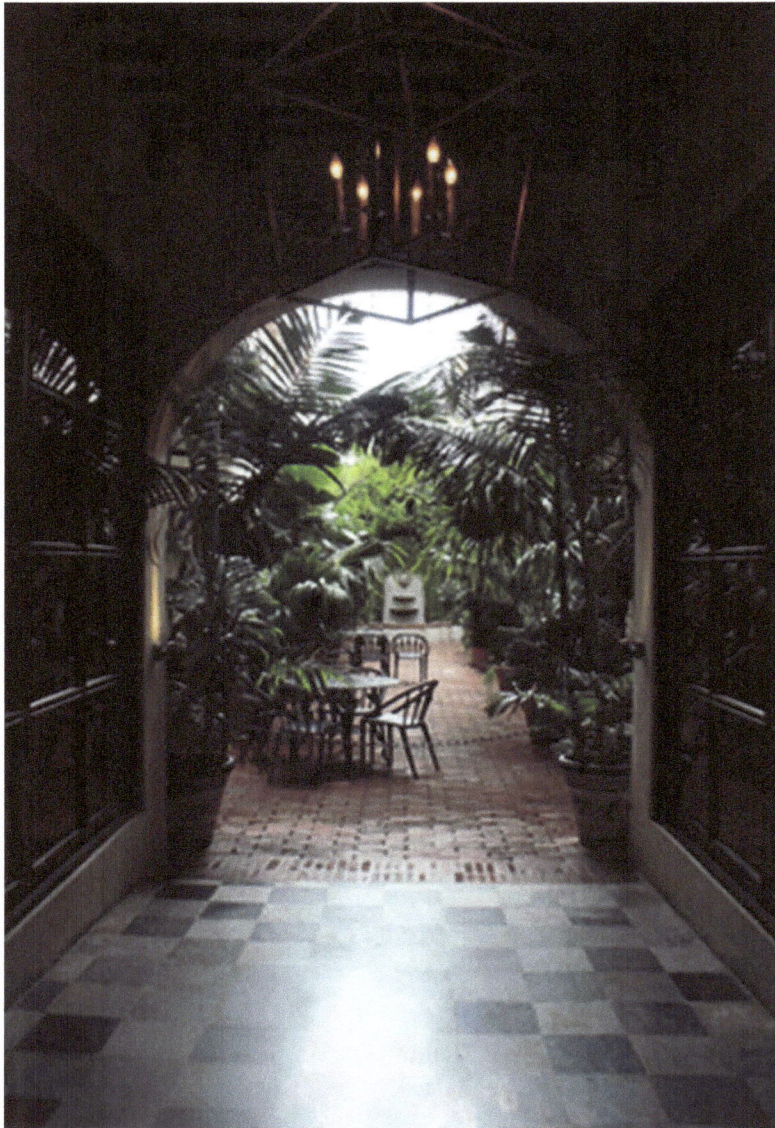

Discounted rates may open doors.

RULE 24: DECIDE WHETHER OR NOT TO OFFER DISCOUNT

At times, offering your services to a client or principal at discounted rates may get you through doors that you otherwise would not have access to. Make sure that the discount you offer is on your services – the hourly or flat rate you charge for your time. Expenses that must be covered in order for the detail to be successful, such as flights, hotels, vehicles, etc. should not be included within the discount unless you are willing to eat those costs.

Determine when it makes the most sense to offer the client a discount. Are you trying to win over someone for the first time? Are you trying to secure return business? You may not always make a profit, but you may win over the client for the long term.

INTERESTING STATS

- 80% of a company's future revenue will come from just about 20% of their existing customers.
- 52% of American customers will join a loyalty program.
- 93% of customers are likely to make repeat purchases with companies who offer great customer experiences.

Make sure to insure yourself or your business.

RULE 25: SECURE AN INSURANCE POLICY

To truly cross over from a paid goon to professional bodyguard, there is almost no more important t a s k than securing real bodyguard insurance. Now you may be saying what in the world is "real bodyguard insurance"? I'll explain.

Let's imagine for a moment that you've been in business for some time now and have made great strides in securing steady work as bodyguard. Your name is recognized among other well-known celebrity bodyguards, corporate heads of security, and even police chiefs inquire about you regularly.

So now you may be saying to yourself, "what more do you need to accomplish?" Then the phone rang. You answer to discover a representative of a successful Fortune 500 company on the other end wanting your services to protect their various VIP's.

You're thrilled beyond belief because this represents your transition to the big time. They've already researched you and know that you're the one for the assignment. When you advise them of your now ridiculously high rate of pay to take on the task, they don't flinch...not even a little. Now you can hardly contain yourself as you continue learning more about the requirements of this amazing opportunity.

Additionally, you're informed that you'll need to assemble your team of protection specialists within the next few weeks. You think to yourself, NO PROBLEM! But before ending the phone call the representative states that they just need two more things from you. "An updated C.O.I. and worker compensation policy." And they need it emailed directly from your company's insurance carrier before the deal can be established and every month thereafter. You're now horrified because you have no idea what they're referring to nor how to acquire it. You've just lost a client before you had a chance to make a dime. They move on to your competitors and you still don't even know how to get what you need to be prepared for the next time a big opportunity like that comes along. Your competitors certainly aren't going to give you this information and your associates don't have a clue and if they did many of them wouldn't tell you as your ignorance on this matter is an opportunity for them to move ahead of you. What do you do now?

You take a step back to make sure you know what you're doing. Here's what you need to know. A Certificate of Insurance (COI) provides your customer with proof of active and established insurance coverage. It is requested when there is an opportunity of liability or large loss. The COI is a simple document issued by your business insurance company that verifies the type of insurance carried, coverage limits, who it covers, the effective date of the policy, number of occurrences, limits, and deductibles.

So, to sum things up, you need the appropriate insurance policy for your business, and you also need to maintain it for the duration of time you are in business. No matter what kind of client you are working with, having the right insurance policy and proof of insurance will protect you and your client and give you both peace of mind.

But wait. How do you get the insurance policy in the first place? Here is something you may not know. In order to get the right insurance for a bodyguard business you may require the services of an insurance broker who can put you in touch with providers who will actually issue you a policy that protects bodyguards. Many companies will insure a security guard company but few providers actually service the bodyguard industry and the ones that do usually require you to have a broker to help with structuring the policy. Your broker will help you to determine what sort of coverage you will need and locate underwriters willing to issue said coverage.

All this may seem to some a big hassle and expense, but a bigger hassle is being sued in court for hundreds of thousands of dollars when all you wanted to do was keep people safe.

POLICIES YOU MAY NEED AS A BODYGUARD

- General liability
- Commercial auto
- Non-owned auto liability
- Worker's compensation
- Professional liability
- Errors and omissions

Consult with our insurance carrier to determine the proper coverage for you or your organization.

Before you can protect others, you must protect yourself.

Do not be afraid to request regular meals.

RULE 26: BODYGUARD AND HIS MEAL

A bodyguard assigned to work a protection detail may end up working as many as 20+ hours a day or as little as 1 hour. It will usually depend on the itinerary of your principal. If you expect that you're going to be on the move for an extended period, you may want to include in your Master Service Agreement (M.S.A.) a requirement that you and any other members of your team assigned to the detail be afforded a break to eat breakfast, lunch, and dinner. The cost of these meals should be at the client's expense. The only exception to this rule is if the client has already paid you an abnormally large amount of money for the job and you don't want to irritate them.

Don't be afraid to ask (not insist). Many bodyguards are either big guys or active gym goers and may require regular meals to maintain the size and energy necessary to work long hours. You don't want to be distracted by hunger when you should be focusing on keeping your principal(s) safe. Also consider that some people in our industry have certain medical conditions that require them to eat at certain intervals to maintain good health and energy.

When you are afforded time and money for a meal you may need to consume your meal quickly to prevent gaps in your security measures. Never take breaks at the same time each day. Eat foods that will give you much needed energy and never overeat causing you to become drowsy.

You will almost always be the one to bring this up as not many clients/ principals even consider that you require meals throughout the day just as they do.

AN EXAMPLE:

On one occasion my team and I were assigned to provide protection for a Bride and Groom at their wedding. The family was very wealthy and rented a large theater for the nuptials. Everything went as planned except one thing: the agreed-upon meals. The bride and groom were busy enjoying their night. Hours passed by and no one approached my team with the agreed-upon meals. So, we waited and watched the guests and even the wait staff enjoy a meal. It was at that moment that I had to think of my team. These huge guys who work for our company require a lot of food, and they were hungry.

I went to the head steward and made a polite request for meal plates for my guys. The staff was very eager to accommodate our request. We ate in a one man at a time rotation, and we ate very well. That would not have happened if I hadn't made the meal a requirement in the MSA or stepped in to make sure the requirement was met.

INTERESTING STATISTIC

Hunger can reduce attention span and performance by 46%*
*According to Edutopia

Make sure to manage expenses and per diems.

RULE 27: REQUEST EXPENSES AND PER DIEMS

When quoting your price for a future detail, be sure to include expenses and per diem.

EXPENSES

The expenses of a professional bodyguard can often exceed that of your income. Potential clients are usually clear about why they want a bodyguard and their expectations of you. It is your responsibility to extract from your initial call the cost of doing business. These costs are typically the client's responsibility, but it is up to you to include these costs in your initial quote and the Statement of Work. This is your time to express your expectations. The only exceptions to this are if its specified in the MSA that your pay encompasses expenses, or you've been granted an expense account with a corporate spending card or allowance. Examples of expenses are as follows:

- Travel (Ground, Air, Sea Transportation).

- Hotel and other housing.

- Occasionally clothing (i.e., designer tuxedos, gowns, shoes)

- For special occasions where the client requires you to dress accordingly.

- Any additional equipment or gear required for the detail.

- And more.

PER DIEMS

According to Phillips Technical Consulting, LLC, Per Diem is a daily allowance provided to you, to pay for logging, food, and travel for the duration of an assignment. Per Diem rates differ from state to state and are not always available when traveling internationally.

There are two types of per diems. The first focuses on lodging per month which is based on the county you are in. This indicates the rate of per diem/per day based on the month of the year. The second is the Meals and Incidentals Breakdown. This is the full daily amount received for a single calendar day of travel. It would be wise to keep exact records of expenses and any expenses that aren't covered as they may qualify as tax write-offs.

HELPFUL HINTS

It's worth noting that per diem rates can differ significantly from one organization to another, and they may also vary based on the traveler's rank, destination, and the duration of the trip. Additionally, some organizations may set separate per diem rates for meals and accommodation or may provide a lump sum per diem that covers all expenses.

To get the most accurate and up-to-date information about global per diem rates, it is best to consult the specific policies of the organization or government agency in question, as well as any travel regulations applicable to your situation.

High-end luxury hotel accommodations are common.

RULE 28: PREDETERMINE HOTEL ACCOMODATIONS

A subject that may not be considered often is that of hotel accommodation. As a bodyguard protecting one's client you don't want to find yourself separated from your principal.

Unfortunately, some clients may not want to spend the amount of money needed to house you and/or your team in the same expensive environment as the principal. I've observed on occasion where a principal that requires a five- diamond accommodation be placed in one hotel, whilst their security team and entourage be placed in a hotel of slightly less grandeur ten blocks away.

If it is at all in your power or a concern of yours then make it known before you hit the road with your principal. Bringing up this topic later than sooner may put your client at risk or irritate them. Be proactive in making sure you're close enough to respond to all threats.

HOW WOULD YOU ANSWER

If the principal will not pay for you to stay in the same hotel, how do you protect your client overnight?

_____

_____

_____

At times, your clients may want you to locate and secure additional luxuries.

RULE 29: UTILIZING BROKERS AND CONCIERGE SERVICES

From time to time an experienced bodyguard may be asked to secure various services for their principal. These services can range from chartering private luxury air, sea, and ground transportation to designer clothing and jewelry. Locating such services can be easy enough. But actually, securing these needed services is a whole different ball game.

PRIVATE JETS AND YACHTS

In today's fast paced world, time is money, and your principal may require transportation options that will allow them to maximize their time. When attempting to book luxury flights and yacht services, you may visit various executive airports or marinas in your vicinity to get information about the types of aircraft and ships available. You will want to determine things like cost, services offered, availability, crew services, age of fleet, size, meals and other amenities.

Before you head out to your local airport or marina, here is what you need to know. Most private air services cater to the wealthy and the wealthy usually utilize the services of a broker or brokerage company to secure luxury travel. Don't assume that you'll be able to show your credentials, drop a client's name and the red carpet will be rolled out. In fact, the opposite is usually the case.

Nothing is more humbling than showing up only to be rejected. Some services are very exclusive, and all inquiries must go through a recognized team member. Staff may view your request as an attempt to gain access to one of their jets or ships in order to take selfies or impress someone.

Others may simply assume that you couldn't possibly have the resources necessary to secure services. It can present a humbling blow to your professional confidence and self-esteem to have a legitimate request for paid services be rejected or ignored. A broker can gain you speedy access to the mode of travel that you require. Attempting this without a broker may result in embarrassment.

CONCIERGE SERVICES

These services may range from temporarily securing expensive jewelry and the latest in couture to the absolute ridiculous. Principals with money to spare may ask you the bodyguard if there are certain things that you can secure for them. No matter what these items are (as long as it is legal) be ready to make it happen for your client. Adding a luxury concierge company or two to your list of service providers will make your job a lot easier as they should already have an established relationship with those you need to secure these items from.

Don't take any rejection personally. Learn from it. These service providers may not have the time or desire to verify the legitimacy of your request. It makes it simpler for all parties to utilize the services of a luxury broker or concierge. You may also find that the rates will be lower as they often time receive daily discounts on services.

LET US HELP YOU

We have relationships with many services and are happy to help you to book them. Email info@bodyguards4hire.com for assistance.

Bodyguards Detroit exclusively provides service to Bodyguards 4 Hire. Here they are pictured preparing to depart on a high-profile protections detail in the Motor City.

RULE 30: BE WISE WHEN SELECTING YOUR PROFESSIONAL ASSOCIATES

This rule is a short and simple one to follow. When you have been in this business for just a little while you may need to align yourself with other bodyguards, companies, and professional associates. Be wise in your selection. The associates you choose can have an effect on how you are viewed publicly. Why, you may ask? Your professional associations often are a direct reflection on you and how you conduct business.

If your associates have a bad reputation or are known for corrupt business and moral practices that same reputation may be attributed to you as well. Seek to link yourself with those who strive to be viewed without reproach, not purposely creating conflict with clients and principals, the press, or anyone. I am not speaking of those who have made mistakes and then later made attempts to correct wrong thinking and actions. I am referring to those who swindle, cause dissention in the ranks, steal clients for themselves, violent brawlers who put the company or their team at risk for retaliation, lawsuits, incarceration, or worse. Those who you do business with will see your close associates as a representation or extension of you and your values. So, take time to get to know your associates well before exposing fellow workers and clients to them. The wrong associates can tear down everything you built in a day.

A SHORT STORY

On one occasion some time ago, a bodyguard requested to interview with me for a position on a concert tour. His resume was very impressive, and he'd attended a known bodyguard academy. But that's where the problem started. He'd attended a bodyguard training program that was well known for developing strong loyalties between the leaders of the organization and the students. Often the attendees would be invited to attend additional classes that the school would offer for extremely high amounts of money. The students would attend these 3 to 5 days' classes with hopes of impressing their instructors and fellow attendees. For most, this led to the promise of work with the instructor's team on tour. This in turn created a requirement for the students to demonstrate their loyalty. So, the interview went well, and this individual was invited to accompany me on the road as a part of his continued training.

What the new associate didn't realize was that I was already aware of the reputation of the school he attended and that his instructor had directly ordered others to contact me prior to his requesting an interview. Some wanted proprietary information about our company, others wanted to know our billing process, and some just made attempts to discredit by insinuating that our company wasn't on the same level as theirs. So, I flew this new associate/infiltrator to the location where the tour would start. I carefully monitored his interaction with my team and principals. He began his attempts to undermine my authority by speaking privately with the group's managers, and then a member of my team, later with individual principals.

What he didn't realize was that I already knew he would. You see, every member of that team was under suspicion for the same thing. This was not a paying client. I agreed to provide free bodyguard services to my clients for a limited number of shows in exchange for their permission to train some and weed out others. To this bad associate, he believed that he was successfully winning over a paying client that wasn't his, but in reality, he gained nothing for his trouble. At the end of the show, he and any trainee that sided with him were flown home and never called again. My clients received a free service and remained free from threat. Of course, I had to make my clients aware of what I was doing otherwise they would have assumed that this associate's actions were a reflection of the type of business that I run. Far from it.

You may not have to take as extreme a measure to weed out bad apples in your ranks, but when you're ranked at the top of your industry, many who are not will attempt to associate themselves with you to do harm to your reputation. Be cautious with those whom you bring into close association with you and your brand. The result of not taking this seriously is that you may lose your clients and a good reputation.

BUSINESS ETHICS STATS

- 59% of employees friend client/customers on social networks with the purpose of future employment opportunities.
- 42% of employees admit to tweeting or blogging negatively about employers.

Big Mark the Bodyguard working out to maintain health.

RULE 31: BODYGUARD, TAKE CARE OF YOUR HEALTH

The bodyguard that doesn't care for his or her own health will not be in this industry for very long. Extended workdays, jet lag, large crowds, the additional demands of life, on stage, sets, and boardrooms can wear out even the most dedicated health and fitness enthusiast. Often you may find yourself working when you feel your worst. You may want to show that you are dedicated to your principal by refusing to rest when there's work to be done, but that would be a mistake.

Taking care of your health and medical concerns will help ensure that you are providing the principal with the best version of you. Also, if your experiencing a contagious medical issue, you wouldn't want to pass it along to the rest of your protections detail, the principal's staff, entourage, or even the client/ principal themselves.

Be considerate of everyone involved. Deal with the concern and when it's safe, return to work. If possible, seek the advice of a medical provider that you trust. Never place your principal or yourself unnecessarily at risk.

STAY HEALTHY ON THE ROAD

The following are some ways that you can maintain your health during details. This is not medical advice. Always seek the expertise of a medical professional.

- Eat a balanced diet
- Take vitamins
- Maintain an exercise routine
- Maintain a stretching regimen

Maintaining your hygiene is essential.

RULE 32: MAINTAIN GOOD HYGIENE

Your personal hygiene matters more than you know. Onlookers are always paying attention to your appearance and the way you may smell. Being poorly shaven or musty just
won't do. Make sure you are well groomed and neat from head to toe. THIS IS NOT AN OPTION.

You may find yourself working in an environment where you're surrounded by the world's elite business moguls, celebrity entertainers, and influencers. Don't allow an opportunity for your client or your organization to be publicly embarrassed because proper grooming and hygiene etiquette was ignored. Daily take notice of the proper and improper grooming habits of team members under your direction, but also pay extra special attention to your own.

Don't drop the ball on this one. Some may think that little things like not flossing one's teeth, thoroughly, cleaning your tongue or using a water pick to complete the process will go unnoticed. However, the opposite is true.

You absolutely must take great care and attention to your hygiene. The time you spend working in a day may exceed 15 hours. Not cleaning thoroughly or applying enough deodorizer may become evident in a short period of time and you might not be able to get away from your important assignment to freshen up.

It's also good manners to be considerate of others. Your principal and others may take offense if you neglect to take appropriate care regarding your hygiene.

Keep it fresh.

HEALTHY HABITS INCLUDE GOOD GROOMING

- Wash body and hair
- Trim and clean nails
- Brush and floss teeth
- Wash hands often
- Wear clean clothing
- Clean surfaces in your work area
- Get regular health and dental checkups

Bodyguards should always maintain a professional appearance.

RULE 33: MAINTAIN A PROFESSIONAL APPEARANCE

The importance of how you appear cannot be understated. Your first impression may become your last impression if you are not dressed for the role you have been selected for.

Standards for grooming and attire should be established prior to the start of a work detail. So, do not assume that whatever is in your wardrobe is appropriate for the assignment. Try to establish an allowance for work related clothing and uniforms, as well as, the cleaning of these items. Remember your principal doesn't have to fit in with your environment, it is you that must fit into theirs. Wearing a used suit that you picked out at a thrift store while your principal is sporting the latest Armani isn't going to cut it.

Be proactive. Look for clothing stores that have regular sales or coupons on stylish but appropriate clothing that will help you fit into your business environment. This includes clothing that you might wear during your clients' down time. No matter if it's a fine tailored suit or joggers and gym shoes, your attire must be up to par. Be the best you possible.

COMMON BODYGUARD ATTIRE

- Suit and tie
- Plain clothes (i.e., casual wear)
- Tactical gear
- Tuxedo

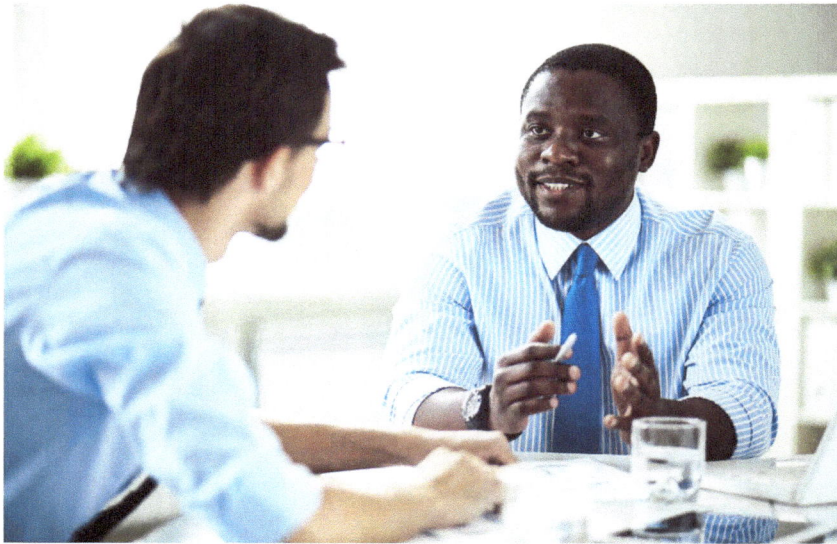

Be sure to use proper grammar when communicating with clients.

RULE 34: USE PROPER GRAMMAR

Pay the appropriate attention to your verbal and written speech when conducting business. The way you converse in your leisure time may not be acceptable in the workplace. Make sure to keep your language professional. This may vary depending on your environment, duration of time working for a particular principal, etc. Take the appropriate time to determine what is the proper speech for the environment in which you will be assigned.

Also, take great care when addressing or conversing with those from countries or regions other than yours. Words, phrases, expressions, and gestures that mean one thing where you are from can have completely different meanings in others. What was meant to be a complement could be taken as an insult. As a matter of royal etiquette, even a greeting that was intended to be considerate of one's position or class can be taken as breach of protocol if done to the wrong person or at the wrong time.

When considering whether or not to pursue an assignment, be ready to ask questions around the make-up of the team around you. Don't wait to be caught off guard.

BEST PRACTICE

Before accepting international assignments, research the language and culture of the region. Understanding the environment and the people you will be visiting will make you more equipped for the journey.

A bodyguard's feet are their most important weapon.

RULE 35: TAKE CARE OF YOUR FEET

It cannot be overstated how important foot care is to the professional bodyguard. Investing in a comfortable and nice- looking shoe is only the beginning. The right footwear is
a must.

You may even consider consulting a licensed podiatrist to determine if custom orthotics may help you endure long hours standing while working a protections detail. This may save you from experiencing pain in your back, knees, or developing flat feet. Initially, this can be costly, but can save you a considerable amount in future medical bills. Being able to be on your feet when needed or for extended hours can equal greater revenue and visibility.

A well-rounded protections specialist will possess several different types of footwear. You may find yourself assigned anywhere from a beach, recording studio or hiking trail, to a yacht, ski resort, or ball room hosting a State Event. It should be apparent that you need to fit into your environment. The bodyguard that is not in the appropriate shoe wear is the bodyguard that stands out as ill-fitted for the profession.

Be sure to take good care of your footwear. Purchasing these items is an investment in your own financial future. When I started in this industry many years ago, I went through shoes very quickly. Today I take great care of all equipment used in the performance of my assignments.

A variety of shoe styles may be needed based on the types of details

you attain.

So should you. A small rip in the stitching can lead to the sole detaching from the rest of the shoe. Damage like this can easily be repaired by taking both shoes to a cobbler/ shoe repair shop. Most malls or neighborhoods have one. There the damage can be fixed and any other issues with the pair can be identified for a low price.

Always select brands that have a reputation for comfort and durability. You can also inquire of others you're assigned to work with which brands and styles they recommend. But test it out for yourself. What is right for one person may not be the best fit for another. Be comfortable when working and look sharp.

BEST PRACTICE

The following are some examples of recommended footwear:
- At least two pair of rubber soled, black, polishable leather and patent leather dress shoes
- Jogging shoes or cross trainers
- Basketball shoes
- Sandals and boating shoes
- Loafers

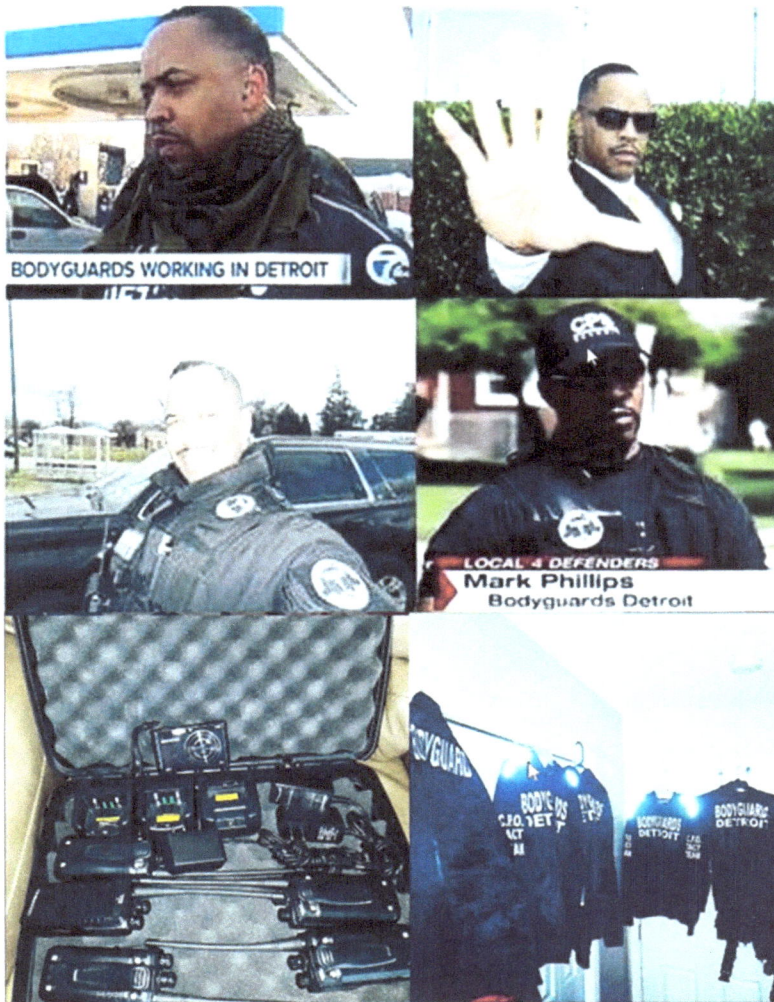

Be ready for any detail.

RULE 36: HAVE THE APPROPRIATE GEAR

A bodyguard's gear can vary. You may have been told by one person that a bodyguard should have a gun and all kinds of weapons. Another person may have instructed you that a bodyguard must have at least two black suits. And another may have told you that all you need is a pair of black jeans and a black tee shirt that says security on the front and
back.

The reality is that the experienced bodyguard's equipment usually varies from one assignment to another. An individual new to the business may possess very little gear. In time the well-seasoned protections specialist may possess many things that fall into the category of gear and attire and may include the following: Attire/ Clothing (Dependent on the assignment, weather, threat, etc.)

- Tactical equipment
- Protective equipment
- Defensive weapons
- Footwear
- Surveillance, counter surveillance, and tracking equipment
- Communications equipment
- Etc....

Before accepting an assignment make sure you are well- equipped. Confirm with your client what may be appropriate for the assigned detail.

SHOPPING LIST

Which items do you need to be ready? Write them down.

_____

_____

_____

Loyalty is a characteristic held in high esteem.

RULE 37: MAINTAIN LOYALTY AND RESPECT

Loyalty can be defined as a strong feeling of support, allegiance, faithfulness, and devotion. Respect on the other hand involves having admiration, esteem, high regard, and even honor for someone.

A loyal personal bodyguard who respects his or her principal can be relied upon to carry out many responsibilities always with the best interest of their client in mind. Careful consideration of how to perform one's duty with thoughtfulness, attentiveness, and civility can aid in improving the relationship between the bodyguard and the principal. The same loyalty and respect should be demonstrated when dealing with your fellow bodyguards.

It is imperative that those you work closely with respect you and each other, as well as, prove to be loyal. Lives are on the line and if you can't trust those assigned to support you it would be better not to work with them.

Never allow envy or jealousy over pay rates, choice of assignments, or anything else to grow into animosity in the workplace. The relationships you build, good or bad, in this industry may last decades and can determine what kind of reputation you build. Try your best to maintain respect and demonstrate loyalty on the job. Be known for it. Be the best possible example of it.

HOW WOULD YOU ANSWER?

What is the difference between loyalty and respect?

_____

_____

_____

Jealousy and contention will break down professional relationships.

RULE 38 (i): THE JEALOUS BODYGUARD

Now you may be asking yourself, "what in the world is 'The Jealous Bodyguard' and how does this help my career?"

Jealousy, envy, and becoming overly competitive in any profession can turn a pleasant work environment into one of discomfort and contention. There are many professions in the world that deal with this issue, but very few where the issues mentioned above can cause so many problems for both you, your associates, employees, clients/principals, and their associates.

Let's take for example, you work very hard to secure a new client/principal. You and your new client have worked successfully together for months and even years. Now comes a time of expansion. You require the assistance of another bodyguard whom you've now employed. He or she may have equal, less, or greater training and experience than you. Some time passes, and you and the new addition to your team work harmoniously together in your efforts to keep your principal safe and free of delays. You've shown this new employee (subcontractor, independent contractor) the ins and outs of this security detail. Even trusting him or her with your principal when you're not there.

Unfortunately, this well-trained associate of yours has now set their heart on taking over this very profitable protective detail for themselves. This may require them to make attempts to push you out completely, keep all your profits, damage your reputation, and bring in their own associates to replace you.

Sounds unrealistic, doesn't it? Well, sadly many bodyguards and business minded individuals experience this scenario every day. Being a professional bodyguard is a business. One that requires you to pay close attention to the title you carry - that of a PROFESSIONAL! Everything you do in relation to your career should be carried out in a professional manner. This includes:

- Vetting all candidates, you employ
  - background checks
  - psychological screenings
- Training candidates in proper ethics
- Establishing confidentiality agreements
- Establishing non-compete agreements.
- Keeping a diligent attorney on retainer

Not many things can incite anger like that of finding out that someone you trusted with not only your own life but that of your principal and their family has betrayed you, as well as stolen your livelihood. Protect your business with as much professionalism as you put into protecting your principals.

Keep track of the names of individuals who crossed that line so that you don't allow it to happen twice. Never allow such individuals to monitor you on social media, access client contact information, or keep in their possession any of your company's intellectual property or equipment as they may be inclined to misrepresent both you and them. Shirts, badges, vehicles, ball caps, business cards or anything with your organization's name or web site on it should be recovered immediately. If you keep your wits about you and follow these steps, hopefully you can avoid having to experience The Jealous Bodyguard.

HOW WOULD YOU ANSWER?

I will protect myself from the jealous bodyguard by:

_____

_____

_____

Bodyguards come in all shapes and sizes.

RULE 38(ii): KNOW THAT SIZE IS NOT EVERYTHING

Here's the question that so many people looking to enter the world of personal protection ask regularly. Am I big enough to be a bodyguard? The answer to that question is yes!

Size does matter in some cases, but for the majority of protection details size is not a major factor. Off course most celebrity bodyguards need to be big bruits but that's because they may need to see over, control, or move large crowds of people in the performance of their duties. Let's be honest, this is easier when you're over 6'3" and weigh more than 250 lbs. But that doesn't mean that all bodyguards are required to be giants. Many security details are comprised of individuals of various sizes, ages, and backgrounds. Your principal might be better served by bodyguards that can blend into their environment and go unnoticed. It's much more difficult to stop a bodyguard that an attacker doesn't know exists.

If you're visible, then you are a target. The bigger you are, the bigger the target you present. That simply comes with the territory. Size has no bearing on the amount of training or professional education one may have attained in this industry. The big bodyguard might be the most experienced and the smaller bodyguard may be the most skillful. Don't allow assumptions about size to prevent you from seeking out assignments that you qualify for. You don't need to be 6'8" to sweep a room for listening devices. You don't need to be huge to be the driver. It doesn't matter how big or small you are when operating a surveillance system.

Size definitely isn't a factor if you're the one writing the checks. Become the professional that you're meant to be. Seen or unseen, you're important. Big or small you're needed.

HOW WOULD YOU ANSWER?

How would you describe your ideal role in a protections team?

_____

_____

_____

Physical altercation can be dangerous.

BIG MARK THE BODYGUARD

RULE 39: MAKE FIGHT OR FLIGHT DECISION

This is a topic that most new to the bodyguard ranks get wrong. Getting caught up in a physical altercation can be dangerous. Attempting to fight anyone in the protection of your principal can result in incarceration, lawsuits, injury, death, loss of license, loss of clients, retaliation, and a bad reputation. Avoid fights or tackling anyone if you can.

Sometimes overzealous fans of celebrities can give the appearance of an attack. Try to use your training to redirect such ones away from your principal, when possible. If you truly believe that you or your principal are in imminent danger, then you should do your all to get your client out of there immediately, only returning when it's safe.

Don't let anger or pride get the best of you in these situations. An uncontrolled temper can ruin your career in an instant. No bodyguard wants to be featured in the media for flipping out! It is very important for you to remember why you are there. To protect your principal. Do your all to maintain a safe perimeter around your principal and if that's not possible, then get them out of harm's way quickly and without causing a scene. Mowing down others in an attempt to remove your client from a bad environment may result in further delay and or other problems as mentioned above. Be wise. Keep your principal safe.

HOW WOULD YOU ANSWER?

When should you engage in physical altercations?

_____

_____

_____

Bodyguard doing advanced work for an upcoming detail.

RULE 40: CONDUCTING ADVANCED ASSESMENT

One of the biggest differences in whether you're a part of a small security detail or a larger one is the advance. The advance is the foundation of a larger protection detail. An advance team may have more duties than any other members of a close protection team. They are tasked with arriving minutes to days ahead of a protection detail that will have the principal in tow.

The advanced team is responsible for making threat assessments and recommendations. They also plan travel routes, locate, identify, and document the locations of hospitals, police stations, embassies, hotels, executive/private and international airports. In addition, the advance team members may take care of arranging flights, ground transportation, parking, concierge services, meals, sweeping rooms for listening/ video devices or explosives and make hotel arrangements.

An advance team is often required to liaison with local law enforcement, when needed, to ensure additional around the clock protection of travel routes, hotel locations, venue, and airports are in place. A workday for advance teams can be very long with little face time with the principal. In many cases, this team immediately heads out to the next location to be secured as soon as the principal arrives at the previous location.

Advance can be conducted by as few as one person or in the case of dignitaries, A-list celebrities, or corporate executives, by as many needed to accomplish the task.

When it's just you and your principal, it becomes almost impossible to advance ahead of the detail. You may need to carry out some tasks by phone calls to venues, check travel routes for delays via online maps and try to be as incognito as possible. Setting up aliases at hotels to throw off potential threats may become a regular requirement of this duty. Responsibilities will vary depending on the extent of the threat, level of celebrity or wealth and status of the principal. Often those assigned to advance details are the most experienced in the field.

RESPONSIBILITIES OF THE ADVANCE TEAM

- Threat assessments
- Surveillance sweeps
- Explosive sweeps
- Travel routes
- Accommodations
- Venue planning
- Logistics

Bodyguards do not typically work the standard eight-hour shift.

RULE 41: PREPARE FOR LONG HOURS

If you're considering a career in the executive protections industry, you can just throw that old-time card mentality out the window. More times than not, you may agree to assignments that don't really have a set itinerary or schedule. Let's say you agree to a set daily rate of pay or an hourly rate. When you start a detail, you may imagine that you'll work an eight-hour shift and then go back to the hotel or home to rest. The reality is that the people you protect are often focused on accomplishing their own tasks, which in turn makes money for them, you and others. A bodyguard protecting a musician may find that his or her eight-hour work schedule has just turned into a 20-hour recording session locked in a studio or has morphed into one media interview after another.

You are still responsible for maintaining a safe environment for your principal no matter how tired you may become. Don't be surprised if your client glances at you from time to time to see if you're still awake. For some principals, the long hours are just a part of another day of the life they chose. You may need to adopt that same mentality. After all, becoming a bodyguard is a very unique profession and you CHOSE it. Now adapt!

Complaining about working overtime is the fastest way to find yourself out of work and could result in a reputation for complaining. Instead, focus on getting compensated for all your long hours of hard work.

Sometimes celebrity clients aren't as rich as the music videos make it seem. You may be promised additional pay somewhere down the line and may never see it. Make sure that if you don't get paid in a timely manner that it's because you agreed to that and not because you're getting strung along. Some clients may have access to valuable gift bags from awards shows or special events that they may offer instead of cash. Others may receive free jewelry and even luxury vehicles and homes that they might give you access to in lieu of cash payment. I personally know of a few bodyguards who because they were patient with their principals later were promoted to that celebrity's manager. The way you choose to manage the above matters is up to you.

Choose wisely.

HOW WOULD YOU ANSWER?

Would you accept any material items or opportunity in lieu of payment? If so, define your terms.

_____

_____

_____

Potential Client:
So... what do you do?

You:
I am a _____.

When introducing yourself, select a clear, relevant title.

RULE 42: PICK A PROFESSIONAL TITLE

This one is simple. There are only so many professional titles for those who are fortunate enough to seek employment in this industry.
SO, HERE'S THE LIST:

- Bodyguard
- Close Protection Specialist
- Personal Protection Specialist
- Executive Protection Specialist
- Protections Agent
- Protections Operative
- Executive Protections Team Member
- Protections Specialist
- Threat Management Specialist
- Threat Resolution Specialist

There are other titles that bodyguards may choose to use, but the above are the most common. Which one you choose to refer to oneself as may be a matter of professional experience or a personal choice. It is up to you if you're an independent contractor, otherwise your employer or governmental organization may assign a title to you.

KEEP IN MIND

The title "SECURITY GUARD" was not included within this list. Security Guard should not be an option, as many trained professionals make take offence to its use as it is technically a different industry all together.

Mentorship and career advisors can make a difference.

RULE 43: DO NOT MAKE AGE A FACTOR

Apart from being an adult (usually over the age of 18) and maintaining good physical conditioning there aren't any age requirements within our industry. Hopefully by the time you're an older man or woman you are calling all the shots with your own protections organization and have had a full career with plenty of clients to spare.

You can always run an agency from your desk.

WHEN SHOULD YOU RETIRE?

When deciding if you should retire, determine the type of lifestyle that you want to live and whether you can afford it. Consult a financial planner when appropriate.

139

There are times when you may encounter a terrible client.

RULE 44: SELECT CLIENTS WITH CAUTION

It is very important to be cautious when accepting new clients or choosing to continue with a troublesome one. The principal isn't the only one that gets to make that decision. You may have to work many hours with one another, so it is imperative that you be able to get along professionally. If you have issues with a potential principal, then it might be in everyone's best interest not to accept that person or organization as a client.

You both must choose and be in agreement to work together.

This is my opinion.

As a bodyguard, you may need to market yourself in a variety of ways.

RULE 45: CHOOSE THE RIGHT CLIENTS FOR YOU

Often to attract new clients a bodyguard may need to create advertisements via websites, professional networking sites, social media, and even word of mouth. What kind of clients you attract is up to you.

How you present yourself and your services will greatly determine the kind of clientele you receive. If you're in a suit and tie in all your advertisements, you may attract corporate clients only and if you're in an oversized T-shirt, you may attract a younger entertainment-based client. Mix up your look from time to time and make needed adjustments where necessary.

Do your utmost to draw the clients that you're interested in.

HOW WOULD YOU ANSWER?

Describe your ideal clientele. What image will attract the attention of the clientele you described?

_____

_____

_____

Remain approachable when working in the field.

RULE 46: BE APPROACHABLE

For years, the word bodyguard has been likened to being rude, and aggressive. The reality is that you as a professional bodyguard need to be approachable.

Individuals may approach you to ask a simple question or even ask your advice about becoming a bodyguard. Don't be the mean guy. Be professional. You never know who might approach you to offer a bigger assignment.

WAYS TO BE MORE APPROACHABLE

- Make eye contact, when appropriate
- Avoid crossing your arms or putting your hands in your pockets
- Be polite as possible while making sure not to neglect your principal or their safety

An experienced bodyguard can help you to navigate the industry.

RULE 47: LEARN FROM EXPERIENCED ONES

Those new to the business of being a professional bodyguard can greatly benefit from working with more experienced men and women. These experienced ones can help you navigate areas of the job that you didn't even know existed. Pay close attention to how they interact with law enforcement, venue staff, hotel personnel, celebrities, etc... Every second is a learning opportunity that can increase your knowledge and experience. There are sure to be things you did not learn about in your basic bodyguard course. Ask questions about procedures for traveling abroad. If you will require a Visa to enter certain countries? How to handle situations when the principal goes over the time they paid for services.

Even tax issues related to this industry. The experienced bodyguard gets to pass on their knowledge and experience to new ones in hopes of instilling loyalty and respect in the next generation of bodyguards.

BENEFIT TO THE CLIENT

Both the experienced and the inexperienced bodyguard have value. A newly trained bodyguard will usually be very eager to prove his or herself and more likely be willing to take on any assignment. An experienced bodyguard will surely be prepared for what the job requires and have the level headedness needed to guide a protection detail properly. Sometimes combining the two gives the principal the best of both worlds. Someday the inexperienced one will become the experienced and continue to pass on the knowledge they have received.

███████████████████████

THINGS YOU CAN LEARN FROM THE EXPERIENCED

- The real rules
- How to cultivate humility
- How to apply wisdom
- How to see the big picture
- How to get comfortable with change

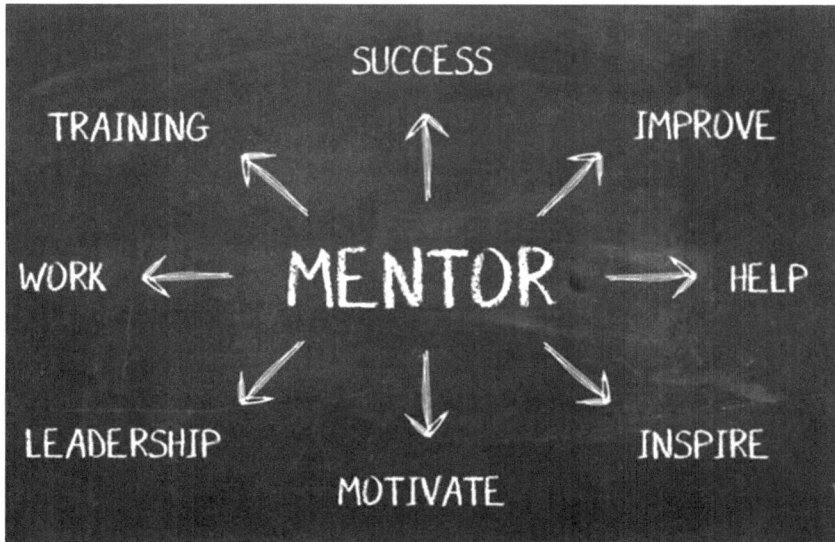

Mentors can help you to skip steps.

RULE 48: GET A PROFESSIONAL MENTOR

The bodyguard that finds an experienced mentor will find himself progressing faster than the bodyguard that doesn't. Seek out those who have years of experience and may be willing to assist you with planning security details or just giving advice.

In the day and age of social media this may be a lot easier for the new bodyguard. An experienced mentor can answer questions about where to secure things like:

- Insurance
- Armored vehicles
- Additional staff
- Overseas travel advice
- Licensing Requirements

They can also help you to skip steps and avoid common industry pitfalls.

DID YOU KNOW?

- According to a study published in the Journal of Applied Psychology, people with mentors were promoted more often that those without mentors. They also had higher levels of job satisfaction and were happier with their choice of career.
- Another study conducted by Gartner for Sun Microsystems found that employees with mentors were promoted five times more often than people without.

It is important that you put in the work and stay motivated.

RULE 49: STAY MOTIVATED

We are at the end of this book, and I want to personally encourage you to remain motivated. There will be times when it may seem easier to take a job that doesn't require as much of you. But take it from someone who has started from the bottom and progressed to the top, it can be well worth the effort.

Having the opportunity to work among some of the most amazingly talented and influential people in today's society, keeping our principals and their families safe from harm and potential tragedy, as well as working in an environment that provides a window into the exciting world of business and entertainment continues to be very rewarding.

You've already invested in your career by purchasing and reading this book. As you later review sections of this book, find ways to implement its strategies in your pursuit of a career as a professional bodyguard. Connect with me and my team on social media, join the B4H Global Network, and schedule a personal consultation so that you can grow and gain the education, experience and exposure you will need to be successful in this industry.

HOW WOULD YOU ANSWER?

What rules within this book will you immediately implement?

_____

_____

What motivation would you give to your future self?

_____

_____

Big Mark the Bodyguard.

RULE 50: BUY MY NEXT BOOK

It has been my pleasure to share with you some of my experience, knowledge, and wisdom. There is so much more you will need to learn to be a successful and professional bodyguard. It took me many years to gain the experience necessary for an amazing 30 years in this business. It is my sincere hope that with my help and the assistance of my team, you will save both time and resources as you endeavor to enter this career field. Let's continue this journey together in the pages of BODYGUARDS 4 HIRE: 100 RULES FOR THE NEW BODYGUARD – PART 2.